Lord Pa
and
Lady Moofy

Krista Dowell

21ST CENTURY
PRESS

PUBLISHING WITH A PURPOSE

WWW.21STCENTURYPRESS.COM

Published by 21st Century Press
Springfield, Missouri U.S.A.
Printed in U.S.A.

21st Century Press is an evangelical Christian publisher dedicated to serving the local church. We believe God's vision for Gospel Light is to provide church leaders with biblical, user-friendly materials that will help them evangelize, disciple and minister to children, youth and families.

It is our prayer that this book will help you discover biblical truth for your own life and help you meet the needs of others. May God richly bless you.

All Scripture quotations, unless otherwise indicated, are taken from the *King James Version*.

21st Century Press
2131 W. Republic Rd.
PMB 41
Springfield, MO 65807
800-658-0284

ISBN 0-9728899-5-7

Cover Design: Cory Barker
Book Design: Jeremy Montz and Terry White
Visit our web-site at: 21stcenturypress.com and 21stcenturybooks.com
For great childrens books visit: sonshipbooks.com

21ST CENTURY PRESS

PUBLISHING WITH A PURPOSE
WWW.21STCENTURYPRESS.COM

Pa and Moofy

Dedicated

It is with great love and affection that I dedicate this book to my parents, John and Ruth Pursselley, alias Pa and Moofy. I thank God for giving me the unspeakable privilege of being born into their home and raised by their love, godly examples, discipline, laughter, joy, expectations, spankings, imagination, encouragement, faith, generosity, and....

Contents

Foreword

God does not call us to fame, but to obedience. Many who obey faithfully do so without the praise of men. Their reward in Heaven will be great. My parents fall into that category, for, while they have not been exalted by masses of humanity, God has used them to quietly influence those around them.

In college I worked at a dry cleaners. My boss was a Christian and he used to teasingly tell me, "Krista, you're a good girl. But the world's full of them and there's no demand for them." In some ways I think there was some truth to that. There are many wonderful Christian pastors, teachers, parents, and mentors who have done many of the same things my parents have. Maybe they have even done greater things, in the eyes of those watching. Though I know the world is not full of them as my boss said, there does seem to be very little demand for them. The world seeks that which entertains. That which is spectacular. They prefer leaders who promote themselves and tell them what they want to hear. It is very difficult for the world to hear the still small voice of God, or take notice of those who quietly hear and obey that voice.

The name of John Pursselley has never hit the newspapers or television broadcasts. It has not been the name that fills great auditoriums, or enlists eager crowds for the latest seminars or how-to sessions. Ruth Pursselley has never been voted "Christian Woman of the Year" or been the favored speaker for all the ladies' retreats. However, everywhere I go, whether here in the United States or in England where my husband and I minister, it is a very frequent thing that I meet someone who knows my parents. Former students and church members, Missourians who have known them all their lives, fellow pastors, missionaries, and many others to whom they have ministered, all see Pa as a wonderful teacher/preacher and a true gentleman and Moofy as a fine and fascinating lady.

Four of the churches Pa pastored were severely divided before my parents went there. God used Pa to heal and restore. During the years he taught at Baptist Bible College he was used greatly to prepare many young men for the ministry. In England he continued doing the same.

I have known many PK's (preacher's kids) who were filled with resentment and bitterness because of their father's profession. Most of them spoke of how their parents preached one thing and practiced another. My parents were extremely careful to not allow that to happen to our family. Though our home was filled with laughter, singing, joy, and fun, Pa was always very serious about his service to God. The underlying theme of his ministry was honesty and integrity. He not only taught it, but lived it. And any time he failed because he was only human, he was quick to acknowledge his failure and apologize sincerely. Moofy was always supportive of his ministry and made a superb counselor and mentor for many girls and women. She was a model mother in every way.

As most pastors have done, Pa has been everything from care-taker/janitor, to carpenter while continuing to teach and preach. We are thankful to one faithful church member in Republic, Missouri for the fact that Pa is still with us. For those who know Pa it is no secret that agility and physical coordination are not among his greater qualities. When the Meadowview Baptist Church in Republic, Missouri was in their building program, with Pa as their pastor, he volunteered to help with all the construction, including the roofing. Bro. Cole informed him that if he was going to be up on the roof he would do so with a rope tied around his waste and anchored to something stationary at the other end. Pa chuckled and told him he didn't need a rope. Bro. Cole spoke calmly and assertively. "Bro. Pursselley, I have never been one for telling my pastor what to do, but if you get up on that roof you are doing it with a rope tied around you." Pa relented and the rope was tied on. He hadn't been on the roof very long when his feet began sliding. He tried to readjust his footing, but to no avail. Groping and grasping for something to hang on to, Pa continued his rapidly accelerating descent until the rope caught tight and held him – about two feet from the edge of the roof. Thank you, Bro. Cole.

Even as they are no longer physically able to handle the pressures of pastoring or teaching, my parents continue to minister by opening their home to many friends as well as family members as not only a home away from home, but as a refuge, mini vacation, or solace from pain and sorrow. My tribute to them is just a token of our appreciation and love.

This book is meant to be beneficial as well as enjoyable. If, while you are enjoying it, you happen to glean some hope, inspiration, knowledge, insight, or wisdom, then it has been successful.

Rutha (Moofy) Early School Days

Secret in the Woods

Chapter 1

"The effectual, fervent prayer of a righteous man availeth much"
(James 5:16).

Rutha Mae glanced out the window just in time to see the old woman shuffling past her house into the woods.

"There she goes again," thought Ruth. "I just have to know what in tarnation Grandma does out there everyday. She's not picking wild greens or mushrooms 'cause she comes out empty-handed."

She swiftly surveyed the activity in the house. Older brothers Dick, Buster, and Luther, were still working on their outside chores. Younger sister, Mary, was slowly wiping the breakfast dishes. Younger brothers James, Gene, and Joe were joyfully making a game of chasing the chickens out of the house. Mama, great with child, was washing empty flour sacks to make dresses for her two growing girls. The water bucket was full, the milk can had been returned to the creek to keep cool, and the left-overs on the table had been covered with a table cloth. Quietly, Ruth slipped out the back door and hurried to the woods in the direction she had seen Grandma go.

Keeping a safe distance so she wouldn't be seen, she crept through the woods without making a sound, just as her dad had taught her. She treasured the too few walks she had with him, eagerly soaking up the woodsman's knowledge he shared with her. At other times she shrank from him. When he was drinking he was harsh and unapproachable. But this morning she smiled and pretended Dad was there with her as she followed Grandma into the woods. Just then, Grandma entered a very small clearing with a large stump in the middle. She paused a moment to catch her breath, then knelt against the stump and began talking.

"Who's she talking to?" wondered Ruth. "What is she saying?" She moved closer, listening carefully. Finally she could hear the words. "And dear Lord, please be with Rutha. She's such a little mite of a thing, and she has such a lot of responsibility on her shoulders. Help her find you and know that you love her."

Ruth sat back, stunned. "I think she's praying," she

thought. "And she said my name."

She listened in fascination for a few more minutes, then hurried back home so she wouldn't be missed. To hear her own name spoken in a prayer was too wonderful to comprehend. She longed for something graceful and refined in her life. Times were hard. Her father had a drinking problem, and her mother more than had her hands full trying to raise 8 children (soon to be 9), and keep food in their stomachs and clothes on their backs. The boys were rough and rowdy, and all too often it was Ruth's responsibility to keep things in order.

Education: A Luxury

Hard as life was for the Billingsly family, this was common of the hills people of Ozark County, Missouri. Education was considered a luxury, and finery was scoffed at. Rutha (pronounced Ruthie), secretly made plans to finish high school, maybe even go on to college. Somehow, her way of thinking just didn't fit into the mold of everyone else. These people had their own way of reasoning and doing things. Sometimes it amounted to plain old common sense, and other times it could only be attributed to southern Missouri, Ozark County hillbilly logic. Rutha's name, for instance. Since the small, nearby town of Ava was pronounced Avie, and the town of Sparta was pronounced Spartie, it made perfect hillbilly sense to spell Ruthie, R-u-t-h-a. Preferring just plain Ruth, she eventually dropped the "a".

The very day after following Grandma into the woods, Ruth determined to make her own prayer place. She hurried through her chores and dashed into the woods. She went to her favorite spot and sat down on a fallen log. Grandma had knelt, she remembered. Maybe that's important. Kneeling beside the log she tried to pray, but she had not the foggiest idea what to say. Finally she simply repeated some of the things she heard Grandma say. That felt right, so she smiled with contentment and hurried back home. Each day she went into the woods to pray, and soon she began thinking of other things to pray about. She felt that she wasn't good enough to be considered "religious," and had no clue how to be converted. Even so, God understood her heart, and already His plan was at work.

God's Salvation

A few years later, two women of ill repute were attempting to make their way from New York to California to "start over." Passing through Missouri, they had car trouble, ran out of money, and were forced to stop. They began scheming how

Moofy as a Young Teenager

they might make some fast money. One of them claimed she had been forced to go to church as a youngster and thought she could remember enough of her Bible lessons to do some preaching. The other one remembered some old hymns her mother had sung to her as a child, and thought she could lead a congregation in singing. They obtained permission to use the school house and word quickly spread through the hills that a revival was about to begin. This was a popular happening in those days. People had little pleasure in their lives, and a revival meeting offered them some socialization, as well as a little religion to help smooth out the rough edges of their existence. Interested in anything pertaining to God, Ruth set aside an evening to attend. Since God's Word never returns void, but accomplishes that which He pleases, Ruth heard enough truth from those two wicked women to come to the understanding that she needed to repent of her sins and turn her life over to God. She went forward during the invitation and gave her heart to the Lord. At the end of the week the two women snatched up the money they had collected from the offerings of those poverty-stricken people, and continued their journey to California. Ruth, however, returned home a different person. There was a song in her heart, and peace in her soul. Now when she went to her prayer place in the woods, her prayers included praise to God for her salvation. Unfortunately, that was about the extent of her Christian growth for the next few years. There was no Bible preaching church in the area and Grandma, though a faithful prayer warrior, had not much more Christian knowledge than Ruth had.

Now her dreams of leaving home and finding a better life

burned in her soul like never before. The year was 1946, and the young girl, Ruth, was my mother.

Pa as a Little Boy

Lonely Days

Chapter 2

"For we are his workmanship, created in Christ Jesus unto good works, which God hath before ordained that we should walk in them" (Ephesians 2:10).

John Robert skipped down the lane toward the river branch that ran through his father's property at the foot of the hill. He felt good today and the cool water offered an escape from the Missouri heat and humidity. Shedding his patched overalls, he eagerly jumped in. The refreshing water washed away his feelings of loneliness he so often had to deal with, as well as cooling his sweltering flesh. It also took his mind off the discord that so often described the Pursselley household. His parents argued a lot and being an only child left John to deal with his sorrow and fear alone. But today he would not think about all that. He would just enjoy the cool branch. Maybe one of the Ruzicka boys would come along and join him. If not, Bob-dog was there. John's best friends were his pets. Bob was the kind of dog that captured a boy's heart and never let it go. Faithful companion, loyal friend, play-mate, protector, Bob was by John's side for ten years. John would never forget the day he had run out into the field to count the brood of baby guinea fowl. His dad had shouted after him,

"You better look out for that guinea rooster!"

"I'm not scared of that rooster!" John shouted back over his shoulder. Fascinated with the multitude of babies, he crept close enough to start counting.

"One, two, three..." That was enough. Sensing danger, the over-protective guinea father landed squarely on John's shoulders and proceeded to give him a proper flogging. Scratching, pecking, and beating, the rooster wasn't about to turn loose of the captured intruder. Then, like a flash, Bob was on the scene. Crossing the field like a speeding bullet, Bob leapt through the air, planted his feet between his master's shoulders, grabbed the rooster and brought the frantically flapping creature to the ground in one liquid movement. What a pal!

Embarrassing Situations

Then, there was Sheepo. When triplet lambs were born one of them was given to John to bottle feed. Subsequently, she became a pet. Cuddly and playful, Sheepo and John had many good romps together. Many of the neighboring children enjoyed playing with her also, but others were not aware of her playful nature. Charlie Ruzicka learned about Sheepo the hard way. Charlie was one of 18 Bohemians that lived in the next house to the north. There were several children around John's age in that household and with their thick accents and old world ways, they regularly provided entertainment for the small, rural community. On his way to the Pursselley farm on an errand, Charlie took a short cut across the sheep pasture. Sheepo saw the boy coming and naturally assumed he was coming to see her. Kicking up her heels she lowered her head and came at a dead run in Charlie's direction, eager for a game of tag. Charlie saw her coming and immediately assumed it was the buck aiming for offensive action upon his person. Breaking into a sprint, Charlie virtually flew across the remainder of the field, cleared the fence in a single bound, and sprawled head-long through the kitchen door. Landing in a heap on the floor, he looked up to see three astonished Pursselley faces staring at him.

"What in the world is the matter with you, Charlie?" someone asked.

"By gollies," he puffed, eyes as big as saucers, "I was coming across... de field and dat old... buck got after me. He would have got me, too, by gollies...if I hadn't run in here."

Then there was the baby duck someone had given him - a memory too painful to dwell on. This cute little duckling warmed his heart until one day when it waddled out into the yard where John was mowing. Quicker than a flash the baby duck met a cruel fate when it stepped unnoticed into the path of the push mower. Horrified, John watched as its severed head popped up from between the deadly blades. But no, no, he wasn't going to think of these sad and terrible things today. He would just push it from his mind. Just then John heard a voice.

"John Robert! Is dat you? By gollies it is you. Think I'll join you!"

"Charlie!" John replied, relieved to have a human friend to help keep him in a happy mood. "Come on in! The water feels great!"

Charlie was always good for a laugh. Just last week there had been an explosion in the night that rocked the Ozark country-side. The next morning John saw Charlie and asked him if he knew anything about it.

"Why yes, John Robert" came the excited reply. "Bill and Jim and me saw a bunch of waspers at the south fence yesterday. So last night we went down dere and put seven sticks of dynamite 'round de nest. And den we set it off. Ka-Boom! Den we went back down dere dis morning and by gollies! - dere was still some of dem waspers flyin' around down dere!"

Sometimes, life was just plain good.

But not always. John didn't usually feel so good. He suffered from a condition called "St. Vitus's Dance," a disorder of the nervous system that caused his muscles to do involuntary movements that left him helpless at times. He was also a weak and frail child from the moment of his birth. The doctors had told his mother that he would never be able to live alone and take care of himself. Indeed, when the condition was in an aggravated state he could not even walk down the street without his parents, one on each side, helping him to force the uncooperative nerves and muscles to do their bidding.   Stressful situations made it all worse, and being around unknown people was stressful to John.   At home, he was able to walk and do his chores and enjoy a little recreation.   But going to town or becoming upset from stress would bring on the embarrassing twitching and twisting movements.   His parents loved him dearly and provided for his needs as best they could, but it was their own rocky relationship that kept tension running high.   His dad was often harsh and unpleasant, and his mother was a very timid and fearful person.   Having accepted her son's condition, she was almost comforted with the knowledge that he would always be with her, even if it meant she must take care of him.   She lovingly called him by his full name, John Robert, and, though her spiritual life was lacking in knowledge, she prayed for her son faithfully.   God heard her prayers.

Bulging Determination

When John was 13 years old, one of the neighbor boys, eight years older than he, by the name of Lawrence Griffitts, returned from his tour of duty with the Marine Corp in World War II.   This young man was a strapping example of strength and fitness.   Lawrence was better known as Jimpson.   As the story goes, when he was just a little boy, Lawrence found some jimpson weed one day, and, yielding to youthful curiosity, ate it.   It is believed that the weed caused a fit of convulsions which scared everyone half to death.   From that time on, Lawrence was dubbed "Jimpson" and was never able to shake the name.   But nobody was laughing now.

Most of the neighboring country boys, John Robert in particular, admired the ripples of muscle that showed through his shirt, bulging in places John had never seen before. In amazement he and other boys watched as Jimpson did endless chin-ups, push-ups, and other impressive physique building activities. John came back home full of inspiration and hope. With great determination, he marched into the barn and sought out a beam he could climb to. Surely he could coax a muscle to appear if he worked at it hard enough. In his mind's eye he saw himself strong and healthy with biceps the size of oak trees. For many months he kept working, starting with one little exhausting push-up that left him weak and shaky. Finally, and not without great difficulty, he managed to hoist up his 95 pound frame for a chin-up. Muscles began growing just as he had imagined, and as his muscles and bones were strengthened, St. Vitus's Dance was diminished. Never to be completely free from it, its effects were reduced and controlled to a miraculous degree. More chin-ups followed, as did more push-ups. Then he conquered the one-handed ones. He saw no end in sight. He would do this for the rest of his life. Finally his dream had come true. Finally he was strong and healthy. Finally he felt really, really good. He had entered that barn a weak and scrawny little boy and emerged a man.

Now that he was strong enough, John began helping his dad with a milk route. This was before the days of electronic milk barns, so the milk was carried from the barn to a truck in large metal cans. By the time he was 17, John could handle a full can, weighing about 110 pounds, in each hand.

During this time of personal growth, a neighbor lady began noticing John Robert. He was such a good boy, but his spiritual life was being dreadfully neglected. At seventeen years of age, John was always polite and kind, but he just

Pa as a young boy

really dreaded this lady's visits. Dread turned to avoidance. When he saw her coming toward the front door he went out the back. His own behavior appalled him and he knew it was because he was under conviction of the Holy Spirit of God. He knew he needed to trust Christ as his Savior, but fear and timidity kept him running. He became so miserable he could hardly stand it until finally, God's patient love prevailed. John woke up one Sunday morning with determination in his soul. He quickly got ready and went to church with the intentions of ending this dreadful condition he was in. With tearful eyes he knelt at the altar, confessed his sins, and received Christ into his life. Now he was not only healthy physically, but spiritually as well. He knew he felt better than he ever had before, but he had no idea of the exciting and fulfilling life that now lay before him. God had many wonderful plans for this strong and gentle young man who was to become my father.

Moofy when she met Pa

Love at First Sight

Chapter 3

"He which hath begun a good work in you will perform it until the day of Jesus Christ" (Philippians 1:6).

When my mother was almost 19, her hopes and dreams unfurled. She had saved a little money (not an easy task in those times) and laid out her plans. Then she waited until she could catch her dad in a good mood. When she felt the time was right she approached him and asked for a ride to Springfield. That was all she asked for. Knowing she was perfectly capable of taking care of herself, he finally agreed to the plan. That Saturday, with butterflies in her stomach, she said her good-byes and set off on the 70 mile ride into the city. My grandpa stopped the car at the intersection of the two busiest streets in Springfield, handed her a five dollar bill, said goodbye, and drove away.

Full of dreams and ambition, Mother immediately got a job, rented a room to live in, and enrolled in the state college. At last, life felt good and things were going her way. Soon she was settled into a routine - going to school by day and working the night shift at Missouri Grill. One evening a young lady friend of hers walked in to talk to her. With

Moofy while working at "Missouri Grill".

this young lady was a nice looking young man. This young man instantly took notice of my mother. Just as instantly, his date paled dramatically in his sight, for what he saw was a beautiful, lively, personable, exciting young lady. His date was a nursing student with an early curfew. So after he took her home he rushed back to Missouri Grill and offered to take my mother home. She accepted his offer and the romance began. "John and Ruth" sounds like a fairy tale couple, and indeed, in some ways they were.

Daddy fell in love with Mother because she was so full of life, energy, and ambition. Following his lonely childhood, health problems, all the difficulties of growing up in an unhappy home, and finally his parents' divorce, her vibrance was like a breath of fresh air. After accepting Christ as his Savior he had become very serious about his Christianity. He served his time in the Army, and now was ready to settle down, marry, and raise a family.

Answered Prayers

Mother fell in love with Daddy because he was gentle and kind. Though she knew very little about Christianity, she knew it offered the kind of life she longed for, rather than the kind she had always known. Perhaps she was acting foolishly, rushing into a relationship with someone she hardly knew. Or perhaps God was answering some of the prayers she had whispered in the woods. Whatever the reason, about 4 months later, they were married.

Mother and Daddy determined from the very start to have a Christ centered home. They were faithful in church and soon Daddy began to feel a special calling from God. This was something he wasn't prepared to think about.

Many of the old fears and uncertainties he had experienced as a child resurfaced. Why would God call him? What did he have to offer? He would need more education. How could he uproot his family like that? What if it was all a mistake - just his imagination? Who would ever listen to him? What about his physical problems? How could he stand before people in that kind of position? Crowds and strangers still made him nervous. He continued questioning and trying to deny the calling for three long years before giving in to God's plan for him to pastor.

During those early years, my parents worked hard on learning how to meet each other's needs. Mother was energetic, strong, and feisty. Some of the rough edges chiselled by

Pa and Moofy as newly weds

her upbringing had not yet been smoothed out, and some of them offered a little resistance. Daddy, on the other hand, had been raised by a sickly mother and impatient father. The Pursselley family was not in the same desperate financial condition as the Billingsly's, but neither had life been easy. Raised on a farm, Daddy was isolated, lonely, and hungry for companionship. The two of them balanced each other out. When Mother was ready to jump in and get it done, Daddy wanted to think it through one more time and be sure they were doing the right thing. When Daddy was indecisive and unconfident in himself, Mother encouraged him to at least do something. That way, if it was right, progress was made. If it was wrong, they both would learn from it. They learned to use their opposite natures for the good of each other and their marriage and family.

The Family Tree Branching

When God saw fit to give them children, my parents both determined to do the best they could to raise us for the Lord. They prayed for us constantly, starting before we were born. When we were infants and small children, Daddy used to sneak into our room while we were sleeping and whisper messages of love and the importance of serving God. He felt that if the subconscious can receive messages the conscious is not aware of, he would use even that means to steer us in the right direction. Mother put her imagination and energy to use in coming up with unique methods in child rearing.

My sister, Robbi, was born during a record-breaking snow storm in November of 1951. She started talking immediately after entering this world, and I am convinced she will still be talking after she leaves it. She was a typical

big sister - bossy, yet caring and protective. The only problem was, I was more of a tomboy than she was, and sometimes I ended up looking out for her. This showed up in
a big way after Mother taught us how to climb trees. I
could spot a good climbing tree a mile away, and it was
physically impossible for me to pass one by. Eventually
the easy ones lost their appeal, and I took it as a personal
challenge when I saw one whose lowest limbs were just
beyond my reach. Their branches were reaching out to
me, beckoning me, no, daring me to come climb up in
their strong arms where I could look out over my world
from far above it all. Naturally, Robbi wanted to climb up
there with me, so I would show her how to get started,
where to put her feet, and which limbs to hold on to, until
she was perched in the location of her choice. We would
memorize every limb, leaf, ant, and inch worm, then I
would decide it was time to get down and find something
else to do until another tree called my name. So down I
would go, back on the ground in a matter of moments.
Robbi, however, became somewhat paralyzed when it
came time to climb down. My instructions meant nothing to her, and finally I would have to go to the house and
tell Daddy that Robbi was stuck in a tree again. Daddy
would follow me to the tree and somehow maneuver her
down. It's a good thing he was tall and strong, because
sometimes I had coaxed her up a rather treacherous tree
to a difficult limb to reach. He always managed to deposit
her safely on the ground, after which he gave her his "If
you can't get down from the tree, don't climb up into the
tree" speech. Before long I would be up another tree and
the whole process would start over. I really didn't mean to

be disobedient. It's just that getting her up into a tree where she couldn't get herself down gave me a sense of control that normally belongs only to the eldest child. It was good for me. I was almost three years younger than Robbi, born in a record-breaking heat wave in the summer of 1954. Since Robbi did all the talking, I remained quiet until I had something I felt a strong need to say. After all, sooner or later, Robbi would tell most everything else. That must be why I had such a need to be the predominant tree-climber.

Little brother, Scott, was born 10 years after I was. He was a good child, just very full of boyness. He had a lot of big ideas and imagination that knew no bounds. When my parents were first married, Mother used to say she wanted 5 little boys. I think she got them all when Scott was born. He didn't break any weather records, but he kept us all guessing what he might say or do next. One such surprise came when Daddy and Mother were entertaining guests one evening in our home in Republic, Missouri. Scott was "preaching" at his pulpit, which doubled as Mother's coffee table. Before it became his pulpit he had used it to cut his teeth on. The cold marble slab on top felt good on his inflamed gums, and it was just the right height for him to pull himself up and practice walking around its circumference while he chewed on the edge of it. Now, at 4 years of age, he no longer needed a giant marble teething ring, so it became his pulpit when he wanted to preach like Daddy. On this particular evening, nobody was paying any attention to his sermon until there was a lull in the adult conversation. Just as it got suddenly quiet in the room Scott loudly proclaimed, "And if God doesn't do it - I will!" Daddy immediately explained that Scott didn't learn that from him, and everyone had a good laugh.

My parents taught us to respect our elders, obey our parents and the Lord, and also allowed us to cultivate our personalities and imaginations. Then Mother's techniques really soared when the grandchildren came along. In fact, it was her first grandchild that sparked the beginning of her grandmotherly uniqueness - the name that all her grandchildren, kids, and scores of other unrelated people now call her: Moofy.

It happened when Jonathan, Robbi's first child, was learning to talk. He refused to say "Grandma." Already my mother had established a special bond with him, seeming to understand him before he could make his desires known. He could speak everyone else's name, so we knew he could say "Grandma," he just didn't want to say it. Finally, he called her "Mama", much to my sister's dismay. So my mother suggested he call her "Mama Ruth." This seemed acceptable to him, but it came out "Moof" and he was completely unwilling to compromise. It later evolved to "Moofy" and has been such ever since. Daddy was named "Pa" and it fit so well he has been called that by people literally all over the world.

As the years went by and Mother grew in God's love and began to learn how to emulate the virtuous woman of Proverbs 31, God gave her a ministry of helping ladies overcome the sin, heartache, scars, and broken pieces of their past. In so doing He has filled her life with the grace, beauty, and refinement she longed for as a child and brought her from being the ragged little Rutha Mae who carried such a heavy load, to being the fruitful, beautiful, godly woman who is affectionately referred to by some as "Lady Moofy."

Back row: Robbi and Me Front: Pa, Moofy and Scott

Family Days
Chapter 4

"That they may teach the young women to be sober, to love their hus-
bands, to love their children, to be discreet, chaste, keepers at home ..."
(Titus 2:4-5).

When my sister and I were born, my parents were thrilled
with what God had given them and were more determined
than ever to have a godly home. There weren't Christian
bookstores with shelves full of how-to books, seminars filled
with desperate parents, or support groups for them to attend.

That didn't matter; they knew what they had and didn't have growing up, and combined that knowledge with some common sense, imagination, prayer and Bible reading. Pa would take us for long walks on the untraveled dirt roads and teach us Bible verses. The first ones we memorized were Romans 3:23, "For all have sinned and come short of the glory of God" and Romans 6:23, "For the wages of sin is death, but the gift of God is eternal life through Jesus Christ our Lord." We were quite small when he started this and one day I remember walking along and suddenly a jack rabbit jumped up and darted across the road into the field. I squealed with delight and shouted,

"Catch it, Daddy!"

Daddy laughed and said,

"I can't catch that rabbit."

"How do you know?" I queried, echoing something I had surely heard before. "You haven't tried!"

Moofy taught us how to climb trees, and how to sit like little ladies. She demonstrated (we never learned) how to yodel, and how to be quiet in church. She led us to put on our grubby jeans and work in the garden, squishing mud between our toes and getting dirt and plant stains under our fingernails. Afterward we knew how to clean up, dress up, and use proper etiquette at a banquet. She also shared with us the joy of reaping the harvest from that garden and cooking, canning and freezing the produce.

Gifted Teachers of God

By far the most important lessons they taught us had to do with God. They read Bible stories to us and played

Christian music. They also turned everyday common occur-
rences of life into object lessons. Everything from the seeds
sprouting in the garden to seeing the consequences of sin in
people's lives pointed to God's goodness, justice, mercy, grace,
love, compassion, wrath, judgment. They are gifted teachers.
God has used Pa to train and encourage multitudes of young
men as they face the hardships of life and ministry, and
Moofy to help and inspire hundreds of women.

Pa and Moofy were also wonderful play mates. One of
our favorite games was hide and seek in the house. Pa was a
little awkward and had a hard time cloaking his 6 foot
frame. He did have a good imagination, however, and would
help us by boosting us up onto closet shelves, or down into
clothes hampers. Moofy, on the other hand, could climb
into the most unthought-of places and surprise us all. It
was great fun.

Another game we loved was dress-ups. We laughed at
the out of date styles of clothing Moofy kept on hand and
felt so grown up wearing them. We would add some gaudy
red lip stick and have tea parties with our dolls and teddy
bears. Often Moofy and Pa would read aloud to us books
like Charlotte's Web, Tom Sawyer, and Little Women.
Moofy even made old-fashioned, floor length dresses for us
so we could play the parts of the Little Women characters.
At those times we practiced our strictest rules of etiquette
and tried to add sophisticated accents to our speech. But
our favorite stories were the ones Pa told about Bob-dog and
one called "Hilda." "Hilda" was a story Pa wrote for a liter-
ature class he had in college. It was about a doll that came
to life. His professor gave him an "A" for the story, but we

gave him an "A+." Ours was truly a delightful childhood.

Of all the household skills we learned, sewing was my favorite. Moofy and I spent hours at the sewing machine and doing hand work and crafts of all kinds. When you spend so much time doing one thing you learn short cuts and develop methods and habits that are not always good ones. Moofy developed one of those habits that proved to be a "tasteless" experience.

When doing hand work, Moofy would expertly push the thread through the eye of the needle, then loop the other end twice around the index finger of her left hand. She would put her finger in her mouth and slide the loop off through her teeth. Biting down gently on the thread, she would pull the needle end until the knot was pulled tight behind her front teeth. I don't know why she ever did it that way, but after getting used to it, it did free her left hand so she could be doing two things at once for about two seconds. Maybe that was why she did it. Anyway, on this particular day, before she knew what was happening, the loop in the thread lassoed a taste bud and was pulled down tight. She could neither untie it nor slip it off. If you have ever had a squeezed taste bud you know it causes your eyes to water. At this point she was experiencing a torrential down pour of tears produced by a tongue held hostage. Finally she called out to me and asked me to bring her the small scissors and a mirror from the bathroom. I did so, then watched in horror as she stuck out her tongue and snipped off the captive taste bud. I must tell you that an amputated taste bud on the end of a string is not a pleasant sight to behold. Fortunately, Moofy is able to laugh about it now, and proudly claims to be the only person in the world who has ever tied her own tongue in a knot.

Seminary Days: Pa, Moofy, Robbi, Me

California, Here we Come
Chapter 5

"Abstain from all appearance of evil" (I Thessalonians 5:22).

When Pa finally surrendered to preach he knew he needed to further his education and prepare himself for the ministry to which God had called him. Together he and Moofy

decided to move our family to California where he would attend Golden Gate Baptist Theological Seminary.

I remember the three years there as being very good. Robbi and I had piano lessons from a student teacher. We would walk across the campus to the educational building where the lady we idolized taught us. When we walked back home it was late enough in the evening the weather changed a little. We were facing the mountains and each evening when we walked, we watched the fog roll in. It started in one or two big mounds coming up over the mountain, followed by a couple more mounds. In our imagination these mounds were the fingers of a giant moving very slowly on his way over the mountains to get us. Soon a much bigger mound would appear and this was the giant's head. Our goal was to reach home before the giant's body appeared and the fog settled over the valley. We always made it in the nick of time, chilly, and deliciously scared.

On the campus was a park area where grew an abundance of buckeye trees. They were huge trees with low limbs - perfect for climbing. Moofy took us there often, on her days off from working at a bank, and taught us how to climb the trees. She also took us for walks in nearby fields full of poppies and blue bells. It was a lovely time.

Following Seminary days, Pa pastored a church in central California. He had a good ministry there, and we had many friends. There was one man, however, who tried to carry friendship a little too far. Mr. Winters was an upper middle-aged man who liked to flirt with the pretty young women. His tiny, impeccable wife lived with his behavior in exchange for the very affluent life style he provided. Moofy was beginning to realize that his attention had been turned on her, in very subtle ways, so she did her best to avoid him. She didn't want to confront him, because that could stir up trouble in the church. She kind of enjoyed using psychological manipulation to deal with certain situations anyway, so she put her mind to work on how to handle this one. Her opportunity came at Christmas time.

A Strange Gift

Mr. Winters approached her after church one evening and asked for a favor. He gave her a rather hefty sum of money and asked her to buy a Christmas present for him to give to his wife with half the money. The other half she could spend on herself. This proposition sent her two messages. The first message was that he didn't care to invest any thought, consideration, or love into the gift he gave his own wife. The other message was that he wanted to meet one of the needs of this pretty young pastor's wife by supplying her with some spending money. She had no intention of spending a penny of the money on herself, but she did agree to buy a present for his wife.

After much shopping and searching she came up with what she felt was the perfect gift for Mrs. Winters. She instructed Mr. Winters to take his wife out to eat at a specified time so she could place the gift in a conspicuous place in the living room so that Mrs. Winters would see it immediately when they returned home. He agreed, and the plan was set in motion. Moofy set the gift in a prominent location straight across from the front door. She longed to hide so she could see the looks on their faces when they saw it, but that was out of the question; Mrs. Winters must not know that anyone other than her husband had anything to do with this.

When Mr. and Mrs. Winters entered their home that evening, the gift that awaited them was not exactly what Mr. Winters had anticipated. Standing there between two chairs was a 4 foot statue that was supposed to represent the biblical "Rachel at the well." However, I have serious doubts that Rachel would have dressed in such a way as to reveal things that are normally kept covered. This concrete Rachel's robe was draped over one shoulder in a rather risqué fashion and flowed down her body so as to reveal its graceful lines in quite a provocative manner. She held on her shoulder a huge basket full of too brightly colored flowers and glittery looking grapes. The ill-mannered plastic flowers were protruding out the top of the basket and the grapes were cascading down over the edges. The whole thing was completely distasteful and gaudy.

I can only imagine the looks of horror on the faces of Mr. and Mrs. Winters. I'm sure she was wondering what on earth had possessed her husband to buy such a freak. Not only was it ugly, but the whole style was in complete opposition to the decor of the entire house. And he was wondering how on earth he was supposed to explain it all without revealing that another woman had purchased this atrocity and given it to her in his name. Needless to say, Mr. Winters never asked Moofy for another favor, and was much more careful about what direction he turned his flirtations.

Room: to be a Lady

Moofy's methods usually are effective, and she has practiced this art all down through the years. When the farm house was built, many years later, Moofy decided to have one of the bedrooms turned into a "sitting room." Since a great deal of her time was spent on a tractor, behind a tiller, or in the tick infested fields, she felt a need to have a place where she could sit and at least pretend to be lady-like. All the girls in the family loved this little room. Her Victorian style furniture fit perfectly and it provided a lovely place for the ladies to gather when they had company. It was not unusual to find several of us with our muddy shoes left at the front door, sitting on the rose colored chairs, sipping tea and discussing such feminine subjects as how wet we got the night before when we had to go out in the rain to help pull a calf, or how much blood spurted out when we stomped the big gray tick we found on the dog. Yes, this room definitely added some class and culture to our farm life.

One day Moofy decided she wanted a shelf hung on the wall of the sitting room to display some of her dainty little figurines. She asked Pa and Scott to please hang it for her. Now, Moofy was perfectly capable of hanging the shelf herself, but occasionally we all feel a need to be pampered a little. Moofy was struck with a desire to be helpless and delicate, and so determined to have the men of the house do this little job for her. They had a few other jobs to complete first, and Moofy was willing to wait. And wait she did, for the men got busy and completely forgot about the shelf. Moofy mentioned it again the next day, and again the job was forgotten. I don't know how many chances she gave them to be chivalrous and manly, but she began to fear that she might be nagging. She didn't want to be compared to the continual dropping of water found in Proverbs, so she set her mind to work to figure out how to get this job done without saying another word. And so she did.

As soon as her husband and son were both gone, she grabbed a hammer and nail and set to work. She drove the nail into the wall and "oops!" she missed the stud. Pull it out and try again. "Oops!" she missed again. About 12 holes later she found a stud and hung the shelf at such an angle that nothing could have set on it. Then she put the hammer away and waited. When Pa and Scott arrived home, she served them a glass of lemonade - in the sitting room. As they sat discussing the day's activities, Scott suddenly noticed the crooked shelf hanging next to a row of nail holes. Pa had already noticed, but wisely kept quiet. Scott wasn't experienced enough in the ways of women to understand all the ramifications of this lopsided decoration, so he spoke up.

"You got your shelf a little crooked, didn't you Mom?"

Pa threw him a threatening glare and exclaimed,

"Son! Don't you know when to keep your mouth shut?"

That evening the men hung the shelf correctly, Moofy filled all the little nail holes, and now beautiful Victorian ladies proudly adorn the east wall of the sitting room.

Graduation at Last! Three long years of Seminary

Plunging In

Chapter 6

Whatsoever thy hand findeth to do, do it with thy might;... (Ecclesiastes 9:10).

From the very beginning, Moofy has been the kind of person who does things whole-heartedly. She put herself into changing the things in her life that needed to be changed, gave us kids a wonderful upbringing, loved, helped, and encouraged Pa in each step of their lives, and yielded her life to the Lord to do what He willed with her.

At the seminary in California, Pa and Moofy worked very hard for Pa to get his education. Moofy got a job in a bank and helped to support the family and put Pa through school. She encouraged him when he was ready to quit because of liberalism in the school, and challenged him to learn the academics and stay true to God's Word. They were three gruelling years of sweat, tears, long nights, and hard days. Just before the end of it, when they could finally see light at the end of the tunnel, Moofy had quite an interesting experience at work one day. It was before the days of computers, and all the transactions at the bank had to be reconciled at the end of each day. It was near closing time, and Moofy was working hard. Just then a drunk man staggered into the bank and over to her teller window. She must have looked tired and worn out (not that he looked any better), but he leaned over the counter and burped rudely.

"Why don'tsha marry me and let me take you out of all thish?" he slurred.

In view of all she had been through to accomplish their task, Moofy took one look at this unkempt, dishevelled disaster of a human being and the whole idea struck her as funny. She burst out laughing at the very idea of leaving what she and Pa had worked so hard to attain, just to step back into what she had worked so hard to get away from. Her laughter continued as he staggered back out the way he had come in. And together, she and Pa kept on working until his schooling was completed and God led them on to a new ministry.

At that new ministry in central California, Pa happily settled into the pastorate, and Moofy was thrilled to be a pastor's wife. Shortly after they arrived at their new church, they were invited to dinner at the home of one of the deacons. He was a country boy, originally from Missouri himself, and felt a special bond with this young pastor and family. At dinner, they were reminiscing the "old days" and old ways of native

Pa in the army

Missourians, and getting into the mood of the evening, the deacon said,

"Ruth, toss me a roll please."

She picked up a roll and did exactly as he had requested. As the roll sailed gleefully through the air, Pa gulped in surprise and horror, and the deacon burst into a broad smile as he caught the flying pastry. At that moment, Moofy became his favorite pastor's wife of all time, and probably remains that way to this day.

Desperation Calling

Pa also did his share of surprising folks. A young couple in the church decided to get married and asked Pa to perform the ceremony. The blissful day soon arrived and found everyone busy getting last minute details taken care of. Two teenage boys in the church, trying to be helpful, asked Pa if he would like for them to take his car to get it washed. Looking at the dust on it and considering the protocol of the day, he agreed. I don't know what caused the delay, but the time for Pa to go to the church came and went and he had no car. He had already donned the comfort-challenged tuxedo and gone over all his notes, but all of that did him no good when he was at home and the wedding was at church. In desperation, he dashed into the garage, hopped on his bicycle, and pedaled his way through the streets of our small town where everyone knew everyone else. Men working on a telephone pole nearly fell off their perch when they saw the tuxedoed man in tails pedaling along. Neighbors laughed and called out to him. Pa just smiled and waved, and pressed on toward the mark of his high calling.

Two years later, Pa took another pastorate in the town of El Rio, and set to work afresh. Moofy again found ways to win people's hearts, and to make the limited funds go as far as possible. One way she accomplished that was to buy used furniture and refinish it. During one of those projects, she was applying spray paint in light layers when, all of a sudden, the can refused to release another speck of mist. She shook it, washed off the tip, and tried again. Still nothing. Finally, she pulled the spotless tip off the can, took a toothpick, and before thinking twice she stuck it down in the tiny tube protruding from the top of the can, and the spray shot straight up into her face. Why it didn't work with the tip in place nobody knows, but it sure worked with the toothpick. Moofy's face was totally white with a thick layer of oil-based paint and she knew immediately she was in trouble. With her eyes burning and her skin rapidly getting stiff, she screamed for Pa. It couldn't be washed off with water, and paint remover was out of the question. There was no paint thinner available, so they finally settled on gasoline. Poor Moofy got her entire face scrubbed until her skin was blistered and painful. Then her eyes were gently washed with clear water and her hair scrubbed clean. After she recuperated, the paint can went into the trash, and the project was eventually finished by brush. I think that helped her understand that jobs don't always have to be finished immediately. Some things can wait.

Some things, on the other hand, can't wait. When Scott was almost 3 years old we were living in Republic, Missouri, where Pa was pastor of First Baptist Church. One morning, Scott was impatiently waiting for breakfast, which was his usual manner at meal time, and he was voicing his displeasure with loud crying. Spying a glass of juice on the table, he took a swallow. Still crying, the juice was sucked right down his windpipe and he was instantly choked. Moofy calmly patted him on his back, then his chest. As his face began turning red she patted a little more vigorously. When his color began showing shades of purple and blue, she patted, shook, turned him upside down and all other directions.

Nothing did any good and the situation was getting quite tense. I was reviewing what I had learned about artificial respiration at school and getting more frightened by the second. Then Moofy had another idea. Eighteen inches of new snow lay on the ground. In one swift motion, she slid open the patio door, jerked Scott's t-shirt off, and literally threw him outside into a soft, fluffy snow drift. The shock of suddenly being immersed in the icy coldness made him gasp harder than ever before, and cleared the airways, allowing life sustaining oxygen to once again enter his lungs. Moofy's new method of projectile resuscitation may have been a bit unorthodox, but it worked. She quickly retrieved him from the snow, then we all sat down with a big case of weak trembles.

Moofy enjoying her two little daughters

Moofy's Gardens
Chapter 7

"She considereth a field, and buyeth it: with the fruit of her hands she planteth a vineyard" (Proverbs 31:16).

When Pa was two years old, he inherited the ranch he was raised on from his great uncle. Pa's dad ran the ranch, or The Farm as we have always called it, for many years, until he was no longer able to do so. Eventually a new house was built on the spot where the old house Pa was born and raised in had once stood.

One year Moofy decided that the ancient garden spot

behind the house at The Farm was no longer big enough. She decided to plant a "truck patch." To the best of my understanding, a truck patch is a garden planted for the purpose of gathering the fruits and veggies into the back of a pickup truck, hauling them into town to a farmer's market early on Saturday mornings, and selling the produce to towns people who don't or can't plant their own gardens. These truck patches usually don't have a large variety of produce, but a large quantity of it. I think that was the only part of a truck patch that Moofy really understood, because an attempt to sell the stuff was never made. However, quantity was planted, and quantity was harvested. Pa and Moofy plowed up a huge plot of ground far back on the east sixty - acreage so far away I didn't even know we owned the land back there. Then we all went out and planted enough peanuts to supply the entire Skippy corporation. We also planted watermelons and a few other things, but it was the peanuts that stick in my memory the best. Planting wasn't really a very big deal, but digging and picking them made a lasting impression on me. It was one of those miserably hot, humid Missouri days, what we call sultry, when Moofy announced it was time to pick the peanuts. We drove out to the farm, hiked across the fields until we reached the truck patch, and went to work with the potato forks. I suppose there is no such thing as a peanut fork, at least we didn't have any, so the potato forks had to do. As I stood looking at the sea of peanut vines waving at me I really thought I could hear them laughing. The rows were endless, stretching over the meadows and through the woods to Grandmother's house, I was quite sure. We worked and worked. Hours stretched into days and days into weeks - or at least it seemed that way. I was completely overwhelmed by the enormous size of that garden. The amount of work, however, didn't seem to phase my parents. It always seemed to me that Pa never got tired. He could do hard physical work all day long and when he came in the house we could not detect one speck of odor on his person. He would be drenched in sweat, but no smell! His pores must have been as pure as his soul. Another strange phenomenon was that when the rest of us would be covered in those disgusting ticks and chiggers that plague the Midwest, he might have one - if it got caught in a seam of his clothing. They must not have been aware of his presence since he didn't smell like the typical working man. But work we did , and that winter Moofy delighted in roasting a big pan of peanuts and sitting around munching while the snow was flying outside. For me, however, the memories of that infinite truck patch kind of spoiled the fun of eating them. I don't know if it was the inconvenience of planting so far away from the rest of the world, or the burden of getting us kids to help her, or if someone told Moofy that a truck patch is supposed to be sold, but for some reason, she never planted one again.

Fertilized Location

The following spring, Moofy decided that the faithful old garden spot was beginning to grow tired after several hundred years of use, so she found a new location. We all knew this was the best place that could have been chosen, but we didn't know just how good. At her request my willing and helpful husband plowed up a half acre and surrounded it with a fence that will be there until the end of time.

For many, many years an old barn stood at the top of the hill by the hundred and twenty yard driveway. About half way down the driveway the field levels out and forms a beautiful bottom land by the creek. For all those years the manure from the barnyard had washed down that hill and richly fertilized the bottom land where the new garden spot lay. Moofy could hardly wait until time to plant. Peas, green beans, tomatoes, peppers, corn, squash, and every other vegetable known to American consumers were planted that spring. The peas weighed down the twine they were strung up with, the green bean plants were as thick as English hedge rows, and squash plants spread all over the garden and up the fences with zucchini dangling from the wires. It was the corn, however, that won all prizes. Every single kernel that had been placed in the ground grew into the thickest, strongest, twelve foot stalk that has ever grown. The whole garden grew to gargantuan proportions. It was almost scary; but the scariest part was when Moofy said it was time to pick and preserve all that produce. We could have fed the whole county!

I believe it was that year when Moofy grew those jumbo size pumpkins. Robbi was visiting The Farm and wanted to take a pumpkin home with her. The travel arrangements involved Pa taking her halfway home in Colorado, and David meeting her to transport her, and whatever startling things she had collected on her trip, the rest of the way home. Moofy, who has a generous heart by nature, offered her the biggest pumpkin on the vines. The size that garden grew that summer, you can imagine the size of the pumpkin they chose. Pa was driving a little Dodge Omni at the time. He took one look at the selected veggie and said forget it. But Robbi and Moofy persistently pushed, prodded, turned, and finagled, holding their mouths just right, until the stubborn thing slid into the hatch back and settled into place. Robbi packed the rest of her belongings and they headed toward Colorado. David was happy to have his wife back and gladly fetched her baggage. Then he saw the pumpkin. The look on his face was well worth the effort of shoving the monstrous thing into the tiny car. Poor David had to help get it out - both then and again when he got home. Robbi chatted happily while the job was being done, and off they went home.

Success meets Poison Ivy

I think the garden story to top them all is the one about the place we had in Springfield. A few years before Ken and I were married, Pa and Moofy bought a brand new house in town. The developer had purchased a large field, and built a subdivision on it. Apparently he had put just enough top soil down to put in a decent looking yard. But when Moofy decided she needed a garden in the back yard, we discovered what lay under that beautiful black top soil. We didn't own a tiller, but we had a shovel and hoe. So Moofy and I, armed with not so much as a pair of work gloves, set out to dig up a garden spot. We chopped up the ground with the shovel and hoe, then threw the up-turned rocks into a bucket. This seemed to be working fine until we found that one end of the garden had at one time been a large area of bushes, or vines, or something. The plants were gone, but the roots were still at home, hiding under the deceptive top soil. Had we been a couple weeks later on our project, I'm sure they would have made their presence known, but we beat them to it. After the hoeing, shoveling, and picking up rocks, our hands were scratched, scraped, and blistered. And now we had to pull those stubborn roots out of the ground so our little seeds would stand a chance of sprouting. That evening, with our backs aching and our hands throbbing, we drug ourselves into the house and collapsed into our favorite chairs. Exhausted and sore, we felt good because of our accomplishments, and looked forward to reaping the benefits of our labor. The next day, however, our outlooks changed. We made the sickening discovery that those obnoxious roots we pulled out of the ground had belonged to poison ivy, or oak. Not only did we touch it, we grabbed hold tightly, gripped it and ground it into the scraped-up skin on the palms of our hands and between our fingers. If you have ever had a single eruption of poison ivy, you can imagine the agony of the deep blisters we had. We couldn't touch or handle anything for days. Mine was bad enough, but Moofy hurt herself even more. Finding she was out of Clorox, she scrubbed her hands in Oxydol, which only burned and irritated the already painful condition of her skin. Eventually the garden was planted and the produce consumed, but not without unfond memories of swollen, itchy, blistered hands.

Moofy and Pa have always enjoyed a wide variety of vegetables as well as all other kinds of foods. Gooseberries, persimmons, mulberries, wild greens, and mushrooms all grow in the Missouri wild and are delicious treats. We have also consumed beef brains, as well as other organs, and frog legs. Being raised that way I have made a practice of trying new things, including alligator tails, turtle soup, squid and calf fries. If you don't know what calf fries are, ask a west Kansas cattle rancher.

Moofy and the oldest grandson, Jonathan

Moofy's Methods

Chapter 8

"Train up a child in the way he should go : and when he is old, he will not depart from it" (Proverbs 22:6).

Moofy has taken the opportunity to teach her grand-children many of the lessons she learned as a child. After I was grown and married, at one time my family stayed with Pa and Moofy for several months. During this time she helped in our homeschooling endeavors by teaching history and science to my children, Rachel and Eli. The great outdoors was their science lab and the things she had learned from her father were passed down to my kids. History came to life with Moofy's imagination and knowledge. She also taught them many fun things from years gone by. My kids still enjoy picking wild greens for supper and have many fond memories of climbing up hickory saplings with Moofy. The idea there is to pick out a young tree just the right size to support your weight until you climb to the top. Then you hang on tight and swing your weight out away from the tree and it will bend over far enough to deposit you safely on the ground. Turn loose and it springs back up ready for the next ride. She also taught them to find wild grape vines hanging from the trees and swing like Tarzan. I don't know if she demonstrated the famous Tarzan "yell" or not, but I'm sure Eli tried to master it, anyway. Crossing the creek on slippery stepping stones, climbing through barbed wire fences while spreading the strands wide apart, and searching out edible berries were some of the many skills she taught them on their nature hikes. They value every moment they have spent with this special grandmother.

While raising our kids, my sister and I have both had times when confronting a strong-willed child just about had us at our proverbial wit's end. It's a good idea to seek advice when meeting a child head on, and we felt privileged to have our own Moofy to help us. Sometimes she was on the scene when we needed her and sometimes it was by long distance. I can remember specific incidences with all six of the older grandchildren.

My sister Robbi and her family 1990

Imagination: Problem of Lying

When Robbi's eldest son was in grade school, he suddenly became quite adept at lying. At first they weren't very convincing lies, since most of them were far too unrealistic to be believed. Little boys tell "whoppers" sometimes, but when his whoppers took a more serious turn, his parents took a more serious turn, as well. They tried all the usual techniques to get him to stop lying. Nothing seemed to do any good. Finally, in frustration and desperation, Robbi asked Moofy to talk with Jonathan and see if she could get anywhere with him. Moofy accepted the challenge and had her talk. Of course she discussed how the Holy Spirit is grieved when we sin, and as Christians, lying can destroy our testimony. As they conversed she realized that his problem was mainly due to a very active imagination, and stopping was going to be a struggle. So she made a deal with him. If he would promise to tell the truth all the rest of the time, they would set aside Friday to be their day to lie. Every Friday they would write a letter to each other and see who could come up with the biggest lie, but he absolutely must tell the truth all the rest of the time. He agreed, and the two of them spent several months writing each other about sneezes that froze in mid air and broke into pieces on the ground, mosquitoes big enough to shoot with a .22 rifle, and no telling what else. Jonathan kept his promise, telling the truth all the rest of the time and pouring all his imagination into those Friday letters. Eventually, the letters began coming less frequently and then stopped. Today Jonathan is a fine Christian man who always tells the truth.

When our daughter, Rachel, was 5 years old she suddenly started writing on the bathtub with a crayon. She had never done anything like that before, and I was shocked. I scolded her and made her clean it off. That was quite a job and I was sure it would be incentive never to do it again. Wrong! She did do it again and this time I spanked her for disobeying me and made her clean it off again. Much to my dismay, she did it the third time. My husband, Ken, and I were at a loss. A little scolding or spanking had always done the trick with her, but she seemed to have some sort of a bathtub obsession. I called Moofy. At her suggestion I purchased a hand mirror. I told Rachel it was hers and she could write on it all she wanted to and be in no trouble. The crayon marks wiped off easily and it was ready for the next time. Rachel thought she had happened upon something wonderful and immediately wrote all over the mirror, then wiped it off. She wrote on it one more time, then put it down and never wrote on anything again. It was so easy.

Reinforce Her Prior Lesson

Robbi came to visit at The Farm when her youngest son, Cody, was about 18 months old. Their visit fell in the early summer during a year when Moofy's strawberry patch was having a very productive season. She had picked a huge dishpan full of the luscious red fruit and had it sitting on the kitchen counter. The kids all piled out of the car and hurried to their favorite pastimes. Cody went into the house with Robbi and her husband, David. As soon as Moofy could get her hands on him, she carried Cody to the kitchen and placed him on the counter top next to that enormous pan of berries. He had never tasted fresh strawberries, and was a little hesitant at first, but as soon as he had tasted the first one, his face brightened and he reached for another. As soon as that one was eaten he seemed to suddenly realize the vastness of what lay before him. He scooted closer to the pan and ate another. About that time his siblings came through the kitchen. They all knew exactly what was in that pan and proceeded to help themselves. Cody frowned, tried to push them away, and yelled, "NO!" He had been privileged in a big way and he had no intention of sharing his good fortune with his sister and brothers. Moofy took this opportunity to reinforce his prior lessons in sharing, but not before she had a good laugh at the expression on his face when he first discovered the joy of a good strawberry.

Moofy's methods weren't always that mild. When Robbi's daughter, Courtnii, threw her baby brother, Jordan, out of the car seat into the floor of her car, Moofy screeched to a halt, grabbed Courtnii, and gave her a sound spanking. Then Jordan received his own a few years later when Moofy caught him in direct disobedience, jumping on the bed. Again a spanking did the job. Moofy firmly believed in consistently administering a punishment that fit the crime. And she did a good job of that with her grandchildren as well as her children. Of course, there were times when a firmer hand on the grandchildren would have been approved by us, as parents. I guess grandparents reserve the right to look the other way occasionally.

My younger brother, Scott and his wife, Cheryl, have 4 children who are much younger than the other 6 grandchildren. Mary, James, Caleb, and Karri live just down the road from Moofy and Pa. Moofy has gone on treasure hunts, invented leprechauns, slept in tents, and just about anything else the "little grandchildren" ask of her.

The summer Ken and I were married, Pa and Moofy built a new house at The Farm. The place has been a tremendous blessing to our family and scores of friends as, whenever we need or want a place to come home to, we go to The Farm. When our son, Eli, was about 2 years old and Rachel was about 3 1/2, we found it necessary to stay at The Farm for several months. There is no better place on earth to learn about nature and the God who invented it, than on a farm. Late that spring, Moofy decided to add some tomato plants to her garden. Moofy's garden had been in the same spot since the beginning of time, and on the edge of it stood a peach tree that was almost as ancient as the garden spot. All the old homesteads had at least one peach tree, and I believe I have figured out why.

A Function of a Peach Tree

We stripped Eli down to his diaper, took the tomato plants and the children to the garden, and carefully explained to them how we put plants or seeds into the ground, and God makes them grow. We demonstrated how to dig a hole in the freshly tilled earth, put the plant in, and cover the roots. We told them to leave the plant alone once it was in the ground, in fact, don't even touch it anymore. Rachel caught on immediately, and treated the young plants like her precious baby dolls. Eli, on the other hand, viewed the plants more like footballs to be thrown across the garden, or a toy to be chewed on, or a scientific experiment to be dissected. Moofy tried to interest him in some weeds that needed to be pulled. He didn't care. She placed him in a big bare spot and showed him how much fun it was to play in the dirt. He didn't think so. All he wanted was the tomato plant at the end of the row. I explained it all over and over to be sure his 2-year-old mind understood my words, then finally told him that if he touched that poor ragged plant one more time I would spank him. Ah! Those were words he understood. He stayed by my side, doing exactly what he was told, for a while. Then I needed to go after another box of plants. Shortly after I had turned my back, Moofy called to me to look at Eli. I looked at him and he looked at me. With his fist closed around the tomato plant and his eyes as big as saucers, he whirled around and took off running. The very idea that a 2-year-old thought he could outrun his mother hit me as very funny. I really wanted to stand there and laugh, but I knew I had to win this little war, so I took off after him. Moofy saw what was happening and nonchalantly reached up and pulled a switch out of the peach tree. That's what peach trees are for! She must have learned that from her mother, whom we all call Grandma Lizzy.

I once heard a story of a little boy who ran in the house one day yelling, "Hey Mom! There's a peach growing in the switch tree!" I don't know why peach trees make such good switches, but historically speaking, they were the main source of that particular disciplinary tool. Our days of modern technology have brought us the wooden spoon for that purpose, but in the days of yesteryear, the peach tree was the modus operandi for spanking children. Grandma Lizzy had one. She even made her boys cut their own switches for their own spankings. After raising nine children her poor naked peach tree probably died of humiliation. Anyway, that day in the garden, as I ran past Moofy, she handed me the switch like a relay racer handing off the baton to the next runner. Eli was still dashing across the clods, his wet, muddy diaper sagging precariously. I caught up with him quickly, and using the twig out of the switch tree, spanked him all the way back to where the ordeal had begun. I placed the exhausted plant back into the ground and covered the traumatized roots. I didn't expect it to survive, but thought at least it could die with dignity. Eli never ran from me again.

Scott and his family

Trying Days

Chapter 9

"Use hospitality one to another without grudging" (I Peter 4:9).

The hardships of the 30's were largely due to the Great Depression. It left many people homeless, penniless, and hopeless. Some of these people drifted across the country in search of jobs, others gave up all hope, some, with ingenuity, started over with great success. It was not at all unusual for the drifters to knock on a door and offer to exchange a day's work for some food and a place to spend the night. This happened frequently at the Billingsly home. There was always work to be done, and what little food was available was readily shared. Moofy learned the lesson of hospitality well, and it has stuck with her all her life.

All through the years Pa and Moofy have welcomed different ones to stay with us when needed. Mostly they were children. I have 2 cousins, brother and sister, who needed to stay with us for several months many years ago. They were Jennifer who was Scott's age, 5, and her little brother, Donny. Donny was a little boy who thought he knew his own mind and was determined to do his own thing. He and Moofy butted heads several times and each time Moofy won. Slowly she was gaining Donny's respect and obedience. One of the problems was due to the fact that this adorable little boy had been influenced by men in his life who had very limited vocabularies. Being only 4 years old, Donny viewed these new words as a valuable addition to his own vocabulary, and practiced them frequently. That can be expected of a child, but I believe it's a pity when adults are so unmotivated that they never get beyond the use of 4-letter words. It's mentally exhilarating to learn to express ones self with more intelligence and accuracy than what is afforded by those base and vulgar terms. Moofy was determined to clean up and improve Donny's verbal habits, and he was equally determined to keep his habits just as they were. Therefore, explaining to him that these words were bad and not to be used, did no good whatsoever. The scolding that followed the next infraction did no good, either, nor did the spanking and the mouth-washing with soap. Finally Moofy was pushed to drastic measures. Picking him up and carrying

him to the bathroom, she stood Donny up on the counter-
top. "You like to cuss, so cuss," she said, pointing his face
toward the mirror. He looked at himself in surprise, turned
to Moofy and said, "No. I don't want to." She countered
with, "Yes you do. You keep cussing at everyone else, now
cuss at you." He began struggling to regain his freedom, but
that didn't work at all. With her left arm she held him
around his stomach, arms pinned to his sides. With her
right hand she grasped his face with the grip of a farm girl
who had milked many a cow. Pointing him back to the mirror she ordered, "Cuss!" After "cussing out" his sister,
cousin, and neighbor kids alike, you wouldn't think it
would be such a big deal, but the idea of doing it to himself
seemed horrifying. Finally he gave in, looked at himself and
poured out a stream of obscenity. Then he wilted into
Moofy's arms, crying tears of humiliation and submission.
The lesson was effective, for he never cursed again; at least
not in front of Moofy.

There have been many instances of visitors in our home
on extended stays. From orphan girls in a children's home
in California, to friends and family, we kids shared our
rooms quite often. We didn't mind. It was the right thing
to do.

After serving four years as missionaries in England, Pa
and Moofy had to return home in 1998. Pa had been diag-
nosed with Chronic Hemolytic Anemia and Leukemia. Of
course we were all shocked when the doctor explained that
this type of Anemia was actually more life-threatening
than the kind of Leukemia he had. While in the States for
treatment and recuperation, my parents were allowed to
live in the missionary apartment at the fabulous High Street

Baptist Church. They were also allowed to invite my kids, who were Bible college students, to live with them. This saved Rachel and Eli a tremendous amount of money. It also crowded up the small apartment in which they had to imagine into existence an extra bedroom in one end of the moderately sized living room. Nobody seemed to mind.

Being typical college students, the kids had scores of friends coming over, most of whom were musically talented. They brought guitars, violins, flutes, and mandolins. They played beautiful Christian music and sang praises to God. Pa and Moofy loved it. Pa had his spleen removed shortly after they all moved in, and spent most of his time recovering from surgery, which cured the Anemia. Moofy was in her glory - baking pumpkin pies and home made pizzas. Pa

My Daughter Rachel, husband Cory, and son, Isaac

would go to bed early, instructing the kids to keep on singing. He would lie down and go to sleep, soaking up the music that was so relaxing to his body and soul. Moofy didn't want to miss one single beat. She would stay up till the last note was sung no matter how late it was.

Invitation of a Proposal

It was during this time that Rachel and her husband were in the dating process. My husband was pastoring a church over 500 miles away from the college, and though I loved the ministry, I hated it that I couldn't be there to help guide her through this serious time of her life. But it was a tremendous relief to know Moofy was there. I loved hearing her descriptions of how Rachel and Cory's relationship was blossoming. In Moofy's words, they no longer walked, they oozed from one place to another. Not that their affections were displayed in public; but it was written all over their faces that they were rapidly falling in love. Ken and I had been around Cory enough to know we were quite impressed with this young suitor, but Moofy was around him almost daily. She was quite impressed with him, also. She made sure there were enough pumpkin pies and other goodies to entice Rachel and Cory as well as many other financially depressed college kids to keep coming around. The kids loved Moofy as much as she loved them. Cory even gave Pa and Moofy a formal invitation to come and watch when he proposed to Rachel. Moofy called me, beaming. "I've never been invited to a proposal before!" she exclaimed. Cory proposed in song and made quite a beautiful occasion of it. Moofy felt honored to be there.

With the threat of Anemia gone, and the Leukemia

under control, Pa began gaining his strength back. Knowing his time in England would be much shorter than he had always planned on, he and Moofy made retirement plans. The Farm contained enough acreage for Scott's family, who live in the original house Pa and Moofy built, and another house for Scott's business partner and his family, with plenty of room for a new house. So construction was started on a retirement house for Pa and Moofy.

Their return to England in August of 1999 was saddened a little when it was discovered that Moofy needed minor surgery. She went through the surgery successfully in July, but Pa had to go to England without her. The house was going up a little slower than they had hoped, and someone had to make decisions about color schemes, appliances,

My Son Eli, wife Rebekah, and Joel

etc. Moofy couldn't do Pa's job in England, so he left, and she stayed. For four long months she stayed and not only made decisions but also did a lot of physical work. It was amazing how strong and able bodied this 69 year old woman was! Recently, sitting at the breakfast table, Ken told of a dream he had the night before in which Moofy died and left Pa a widower. This was bad enough, but the next part of the dream had Pa remarried to a woman - I won't tell her name - but let's just say it could compare to Pope John Paul marrying Madonna. The conversation got funny at that point, and Ken said he believes no man should outlive his wife. Women need a chance to be their own bosses for a while, then to dream again of a knight in shining armor to come riding for them on a beautiful white steed. Moofy was afraid her dream would have her knight in a shining wheel chair, riding a white porcelain bedpan. The truth is, the Lord has blessed both Pa and Moofy with good health and strength. Even while looking in the face of Leukemia, Pa can put in a better day's work on The Farm than most 72 year old men. And Moofy is, to put it in Pa's words, "tougher than a pine knot."

The house is visible evidence of Moofy's and Pa's hospitable nature. The basement is a complete apartment to house us when we are in the States, (we are taking Pa's place in England) and also has a huge guest area on the third floor for when the house is full. Rachel and Cory are also missionaries and the Farm equals "home" for them when they are in the States. Eli and his bride Rebekah spend many weekends there to receive the respite they need while finishing Bible College and Graduate School. With 3 children, 3 children-in-law, 10 grandchildren, 4 grandchildren-in-law and promise of a few more in the near future, and 4 (soon to be 6) great-grandchildren, it's fairly obvious that a lot of space will be necessary from time to time. Not to mention the scores of friends that honor their presence quite frequently.

Yes, hospitality is a wonderful gift!

Pa as a boy on the farm

Pa's Methods

Chapter 10

"And, ye fathers, provoke not your children to wrath: but bring them up in the nurture and admonition of the Lord" (Ephesians 6:4).

Growing up the way they did, Pa and Moofy both have always been especially sensitive to the needs of children. Today's talk about how resilient kids are after a deep, emotional trauma is a lot of garbage, or as Pa would say, hog-wash. The Bible speaks much about the consequences of harming a child. That is not to say that kids should have their own way all the time. They definitely need absolute boundaries with lots of love and consistent discipline.

On the lighter side of the issue, however, kids can learn to cope with harmless idiosyncrasies that may crop up in the personalities of their parents and grandparents. Pa and Moofy have a few. I'm sure Moofy acquired most of hers from Grandma Lizzy, who probably acquired hers from her mother, and so on. Most of these have to do with curing what ails you. Moofy had worlds of confidence in them. And why not? All 9 kids in her family lived to adulthood, so they must have worked!

Here is my list of Moofy cures.

1. Headache - work it off.
2. Minor burn on hand - run hot, soapy dishwater and do dishes until it stops burning.
3. Sore throat - swallow turpentine in sugar.
4. Chest congestion - swallow a blob of Vicks Vaporub.
5. Tummy ache, constipation, tired, listless, or depressed - castor oil.
6. Poison ivy - rub down with Clorox.
7. Chigger bites - dab with fingernail polish, preferably clear.
8. Blister - keep working till it turns into a callous.
9. Backache - weed the garden.
10. Gas - bend over and spit under a rock.
11. Boredom - clean closet, mop floors, wash car, clean out garage, wash light fixtures, brush the dog, bake

a pie, clean the mirrors, take out the garbage, etc.

12. Insect repellent - diesel fuel on clothing.
13. Stain removal - place in direct sunlight.

I will admit, some of these actually work. However, I have been the victim of some that don't work, too.

Pa's Conservative Techniques

And then, there's Pa. Growing up during hard times made him extremely conservative when it comes to waste. Don't use any more of anything than you absolutely have to, has been his motto forever.

When Robbi and I were quite small I can remember a few instances when Pa was helping out by giving us our bath. He would run about an inch and a half of moderately warm water and make us stand up in the tub. It was easier for him to get to us that way. We would stand there shivering and begging, "Daddy, please let me sit down. I'm cold." He ignored our pleas until he had thoroughly scrubbed every inch of our skin, then let us sit down to rinse off. By then the inch and a half of moderately warm water had dropped about 20 degrees and sitting down did nothing toward warming us up. We were clean, though, so the mission had been successfully completed. Ten years later, when Scott was quite small I passed by the closed bathroom door one day and heard a desperate voice saying, "Daddy, please let me sit down. I'm cold."

We were always required to use a minimal amount of bath water, whether Pa was involved in the bath or not. There was an occasion, however, on which that rule was ignored. Whenever one of us was sick, the bath would be bypassed a couple days until we were feeling better. At the instant we felt strong enough to be up that long, Moofy would run the bath water just as warm and deep as we wanted it. She would put in bubble bath until the suds were up to our chins and let us relax in the tub as long as we felt like it. Then she would wrap us up in the biggest, thickest towel she could find, dry us off, dress us in clean pajamas and put us back to bed. I always thought that did more toward curing us than all the turpentine or castor oil in the world.

Moofy's Gentle Hands

Moofy just had a gentle mother's way of healing our wounds, whether they were physical owies, or hurt feelings. When I was in Junior High, I noticed the other girls were beginning to wear make up, do a little extra with their hair, and polish their fingernails. I desperately wanted long, tapered fingernails that could be polished to a colorful shine. I filed, cleaned, removed cuticles, and tried to stop picking at hang nails. All to no avail. My nails were blocky looking, the cuticles refused to be removed, and hang nails beckoned me relentlessly. I finally gave way to tears and went sobbing to Moofy.

"Look at these ugly hands!" I wailed. "I can't make them pretty no matter what!" Moofy looked at my hands for a moment, then held out hers. There was a remarkable resemblance.

"Look", she said. "Yours look just like mine. They may not be the most beautiful, but they have wiped a lot of little noses, made a lot of little dresses, dried a lot of little tears, and baked a lot of apple pies. I'd rather have useful hands than beautiful hands, any day."

It was hard for me to admit that she was right, but I knew in my heart that I was being vain and selfish. Ever since then I have been thankful that my hands look like Moofy's. I only hope and pray that mine might accomplish some of the good and beautiful things that hers have.

Eli's hands proved to be another problem. When he was just in kindergarten he started biting his fingernails. I tried putting hot pepper juice on them, but he liked it. I tried wrapping the ends of all his fingers in adhesive tape, and I thought that was going to work because it was embarrassing to him to answer all the questions about what happened to his fingers. Then one day he came home from school with the ends of his fingers unwrapped and he was chewing on a big wad of nasty, dirty adhesive tape. It didn't seem to bother him a bit, but I almost threw up when I thought of all the disgusting things that tape probably touched before it went into his mouth. I was trying to decide what to try next, when Pa and Moofy came to visit. I explained the problem to Moofy and she had an idea. She told him that if he would stop biting his nails, she would buy him his very own set of fingernail clippers. The offer was one he couldn't resist, so the habit died immediately. Moofy kept her word and bought the clippers. Eli proudly carried them in his pocket, along with his rocks, earth worms, and empty shotgun shells.

I always shuddered when I had to empty his pockets to do laundry. It is beyond my ability to imagine why boys fill their pockets with some of the horrifying things I found there. I must admit boys can be disarmingly charming and delightful. But they can be equally exasperating. Especially when it comes to potty training.

I can remember when Moofy potty trained Scott. Then Robbi and I implemented the same techniques on our boys. Often Moofy was visiting, and was able to offer her encouragement and support. At other times we were visiting The Farm, which is the most ideal place in the world to train a little boy. Moofy has a big front porch, and it was great fun for the little grandsons to stand on the edge of the porch and take aim at whatever rocks, sticks, and other debris might be laying around in the yard. During the times when Robbi's family and mine were all at The Farm together, the front porch became the regular meeting place for the boys. The only problem was, sometimes little boys don't have the discernment to know when and where a front porch is an acceptable spot for this activity. We worked hard to make them understand just any porch wouldn't do.

It was always great fun to have all the little cousins together. Moofy delighted in making her specialty for breakfast - McMoofy Muffins. She made biscuits from scratch, added a sausage patty or bacon, scrambled egg and the kids' choice of toppings such as onion, peppers, hot sauce, cheese, or all of the above. She also made a cold drink for hot Missouri days called Junk Juice. This amounted to a combination of all the juices available in her kitchen. It usually went something like this. A little bit of orange juice and grape juice left over from yesterday's breakfast, some strawberry juice left in a bowl from this morning's breakfast, a glass of juice drained from a can of fruit that went into her jello mold, and a little tea left in the early morning teapot would all be mixed together. She would taste it and decide if it needed sugar to sweeten it up a bit, or a little lemon juice to give it some twang. There was no telling what putrid color it might turn out to be. I suppose that's why food manufacturers add artificial colorings. But the truth is, the kids didn't care what color it was. They just liked it because Moofy made it and it tasted good.

Another bit of summer fun was the fountain Moofy purchased for her sitting room. Unlike the hideous thing that stood in the Winters' living room, this concrete lady is lovely. She stands behind a pool that looks like a clam shell, and a trickle of water runs out of the rocks by her feet, filling the pool with cool, refreshing water. Having no air conditioning

The oldest and youngest grandchildren 1994

in the house, Moofy would allow the grandchildren to stand at the pool and splash all they wanted to. The floor could be wiped up later with no harm done. On one particularly hot day we found Rachel, stripped naked, splashing to her heart's content and swirling her panties around in the pool. Nineteen years later, for the sake of nostalgia, I borrowed the fountain for the reception following Rachel and Cory's wedding. It added a touch of class to the already beautiful decorations, and a few sweet memories for me.

On one of those occasions when we were all at The Farm together, Moofy even rented a goat for the grandchildren to play with in the yard. They had great fun chasing and trying to ride that goat. And the goat had fun, too, with all those play mates. Late that evening, some of the kids had been called in to get ready for bed, and a few were still outside, playing. As I looked out the window, I saw one kid chasing the goat, one catching fireflies, and one practicing his newly acquired skill at the edge of the porch. Smiling to myself, I turned and walked down the hallway toward the kitchen. As I passed by the bathroom door I heard a small voice whining, "Pa, please let me sit down. I'm cold."

Pa and Moof's 50th wedding anniversary

Later Days

Chapter 11

"Have not I commanded thee? Be strong and of a good courage; be not afraid, neither be thou dismayed: for the Lord thy God is with thee whithersoever thou goest" (Joshua 1:9).

When Moofy took her first step of faith years ago in the woods, God knew her heart and so the Holy Spirit began the process of drawing her to himself. Since then He has been with her through each step of her life. At the same time He continued to lead and strengthen Pa in ways he never dreamed possible. Some steps were easy, and others were real trials of their faith.

In 1960, Pa and Moofy loaded their few belongings in a U-haul trailer, loaded Robbi and me into the Rambler, and off we went to California. Cars didn't automatically come with air conditioning back then, and though crossing the desert in mid-summer was not exactly a pleasant experience, God was with us and sustained us through the vastness of the hot, dry desert until we arrived safely in San Francisco. Pa went through the seminary, then pastored two different churches. Many steps of faith were taken during those seven years. Many lessons were learned. Our family was enriched, both spiritually, and by the birth of my baby brother, Scott.

The day finally came when it was time to go back home to Missouri. We joyfully crossed the desert again. I remember the night well when we arrived at our final destination. Pa and Robbi, in the moving van, had fallen behind Moofy, Scott and me in the car. It was a cold, windy, snowy night. The swaying trees, blowing snow, and whistling wind was something I was not accustomed to after growing up in California. It was spooky and I really wished my daddy was there. We drove out in the country to the old farm house my great grandfather, whom we simply called Grandpa Moore, had lived in all his life. He was dead now, and the house had been empty for several years. I did have good memories of that house. While living in California we had come to Missouri on vacation a couple of times, and part of the time would be spent at that house. Grandpa Moore was a funny little man my sister and I adored. He had an old mantel clock that struck the time, and the house smelled of pipe tobacco and that "old house" smell that I've never been quite able to identify. The large kitchen table had a cloth on it that hung almost to the floor, and Robbi and I loved to play under there. The way the table top sat on the frame left a small gap between them, and we collected things like discarded razor blades and the shed skins from locusts to hide there. There were cob webs and spider eggs under there, but we didn't mind. It was always summer time when we visited, and we could play outside and eat watermelon almost everyday.

This cold, creepy night enclosed around me in sharp contrast to the warm memories that had been playing in my mind. It didn't even seem like the same house. Gone was the old mantel clock, kitchen table, and all the other furnishings I was familiar with. The only thing still remaining was the old, black pot-belly stove in the living room. I had always enjoyed seeing it there, but I had never been around when it was in use. The storm had caused the electricity to go out, and when we entered the dreary, dark house that night I was terrified. Moofy, on the other hand, felt quite at home. She went to the pantry and located two kerosene lanterns. Then she found matches, and soon we had a little light. I just knew they would explode. The next thing she did was search out some kindling and firewood and proceed to build a fire in that poor old smoke-puffing stove. I could visualize the house going up in flames and us freezing outside in the bitter night. However, much to my surprise, the stove was soon smiling with warmth and the soft light from the lanterns was looking much more inviting than at first. I don't know if Moofy realized just how scared I was that night, but by the time Pa and Robbi arrived I was quite proud of how warm and cozy "we" had made the place. That was our home for several months until God gave Pa his next pastorate. It was also a learning place for us kids. Moofy immediately took Scott outside and showed him what the front porch was for, and Robbi and I eagerly learned about the change of seasons and other nature lessons.

A Snowy Imagination

The house had been unused for so long Pa and Moofy were concerned that the water well could be contaminated. So they took gallon jugs into town to bring out drinking water for us. This might have been the first time they had ever left us home alone. We were a little apprehensive, but felt very mature and responsible at the same time. They had been gone only a short time when "apprehensive" started taking over. The sky was turning gray and the chill in the air was biting harder. Soon little snow flakes started falling. At that point, Robbi's imagination took full control over "mature and responsible." She had just finished reading a story about some kids in the pioneer days who were stranded at home in a blizzard without their parents. The storm howled until all the firewood was burned, then they started chopping up the furniture. They ended up burning everything they could get their hands on and finally froze to death, anyway. Robbi looked out the window at the snow flurries playfully dancing around, but what she saw was a full blown, raging blizzard. Panic-stricken, she ordered me to help bring in more wood. She was sure that, when the storm got worse, we wouldn't be able to see all the way to the wood pile, and could easily get lost. So we put on our coats and mittens and carried every stick of wood into the closed in back porch. We left only a tiny, narrow path from outside door to kitchen door. Satisfied that we might stand a slim chance of surviving until our parents returned home, we busied ourselves with various activities to keep our minds off the menacing storm.

You can imagine the looks on Pa's and Moofy's faces when they returned home and found the entire wood pile in the back room. And I don't even like to think about the looks on our faces when we realized the life-threatening storm was gone and the hint of white on the ground was rapidly vanishing. We returned the woodpile to its rightful place outside the house while Pa and Moofy stayed inside, probably laughing hysterically.

With Pa's and Moofy's gentle guidance we began to learn not to fear the elements, but respect them, and enjoy the warmth of the wood stove and somewhat primitive surroundings in which we lived. One day Moofy put a big pot of pinto beans on top of the wood stove, and added a big chunk of ham. Robbi and I informed her that we didn't like pinto beans. They were served frequently in the school cafeteria in California where the cooks threw them in a pot, covered them with water, and boiled them until they were just barely soft enough to chew. Then they were slopped on our plate with a piece of dry corn bread from a mix, and they were hardly palatable. She smiled and told us to just wait. She left those beans on the stove to simmer all day. That evening she made her delicious corn bread from scratch, and served up those beans. The juice was thick and the beans were well done, soft and oh so yummy. The aroma was irresistible, and the ham had flavored those beans to perfection.

We asked for beans for supper every night for the next week.

Winter turned to spring and Grandpa Moore's old home place took on all the familiar characteristics of past vacations. Pa took us fishing in the pond over the hill, we collected 32 terrapins which we released the next day, and we investigated all the spiders, bugs, birds, leaves, and wild flowers we could find. We even endured a bout with poison ivy. Moofy took us to the woods and taught us which mushrooms are edible, and we fried them for supper. They went well with the wild greens she taught us to pick from around the barnyard. Robbi and I were rapidly turning back into the country girls we had started out to be before California almost succeeded in civilizing us. We liked this life much better.

Phantom of the Farm House

As siblings usually do, Robbi and I had our methods of driving each other nuts. She, being older, had the advantage in this practice, but Grandpa Moore's house offered me a scheme of getting even that made up for almost all the mean and rotten things she had ever done to me. This old farm house had an upstairs in it that could have been the setting for a horror movie if the right producer had ever found it. I loved it. Robbi hated it. I played up there until the heat of the summer drove me back downstairs. Then one day I had the mother of all vengeful ideas. I climbed the stairs (I didn't have to sneak since nobody liked it up there except me) and laid out my sinister plans. We had two of the ugliest dolls that have ever been created. Our rich Great Aunt Nina had sent them to us one Christmas when we had asked for the beautiful Patty Play-Pal dolls that were so popular at the time. We cried with disappointment when we opened those beautifully wrapped packages and found, not Patty Play-Pals, but Hilda the Hillbilly with her attached corn-cob pipe, and Tilly the Talker, complete with a stupid little plastic telephone. For the first time since we had received those hideous creatures, I was thankful. I took Tilly the Talker, because she was Robbi's, and a rope upstairs. I tied one end of the rope around Tilly's scrawny little neck and the other end to the railing at the top of the stairs. After carefully studying the geometrics of this procedure, I managed to delicately attach the middle of the rope to the door at the bottom of the stairs and balance the doll on the ledge around the top of the stairs. If I opened the door just barely enough to squeeze through, the doll stayed in place. But if I pushed the door open wide, the doll swung down straight toward my face in a delightfully horrifying manner. Now for the hard part. I had to find a way to get Robbi to open that door. Putting on my innocent face, I told Moofy I wanted to play a trick on Robbi, and I needed her to send her upstairs for something. She was a little hesitant at first, but finally gave in. I could barely hide my eagerness when Moofy called Robbi to the kitchen and told her to go upstairs to bring down some fruit jars. Robbi gave every excuse she could think of, but finally was constrained to go. It was beautiful. On the few occasions when she had gone upstairs she always opened the door as wide as it could go because she would have just died if it had closed while she was up there. I held my breath as she approached the door. Taking a deep cleansing breath to calm herself, she turned the door knob and pulled the door open. True to my plans, Tilly came swinging down like a phantom, big blue eyes bulging, and that ignorant looking grin still on her freckled face. Robbi's scream echoed through the house, as did my laughter. I think Moofy was a little stunned at the deviousness of my plan, but Robbi's reaction was so rewarding she really couldn't get angry at me. The same cannot be said of Robbi, however. Once she was able to breathe again, and her heart was beating a regular rhythm, I thought she might kill me. But I guess she couldn't come up with a plan to top mine, so she simply didn't talk to me for a couple days. I could live with that.

After several months Pa was called to pastor a church and Grandpa Moore's house was eventually moved to a different location. I saw the old farm land once after that. Without the old house it didn't even look like the same farm. It was such a sad sight, I've never gone back. Even that was a lesson for me. Things change, people die or move away, plans are altered, children grow up, and familiar objects deteriorate. But God's Word will never change or pass away. That is the only thing in this life that is absolute, and the only thing that we can actually hold on to.

So, as we moved on, we found that God blessed more and more. And as Pa and Moofy allowed His will to rule their lives, we learned to do the same. Of all the many, many lessons we learned from our godly parents, serving the Lord is by far the most important.

England meets Pa and Moofy

Pa pastored for several more years, taught at Baptist Bible College, and pastored again for several more years. Then he knew the Lord was calling him to a new and different ministry. At 66 years of age, when most people are retiring, Pa and Moofy were on their way to England to help start the Independent Baptist Bible College of Great Britain. This was one of their most challenging and most rewarding ministries. The opportunity to work with future pastors in a place where sin is rampant and the gospel is scarce was both humbling and exciting. Pa and Moofy made a great impact on and lasting friendships with many of the British Christians. Going across the seas to live in a foreign country at that age was quite an undertaking.

Dealing with jet lag and culture shock while learning to

Moofy and Pa in England

function in a foreign country was a challenge met and conquered with style. Pa enjoyed the half mile walk to market and often went there to fill the lists Moofy ordered. One day she asked for a beef roast.

"How big?" Pa asked.

"Just two of us. One pound should be enough," she answered.

At the meat market, Pa asked the butcher for a one pound beef roast. Now, one needs to understand British commerce before they attempt to make such a difficult transaction as buying a piece of meat. In England, one pound is an increment of money, equal to approximately $1.60. What the butcher did next was to present Pa with a roast that was worth one British pound - about 2 square inches in size. Rather than correct his mistake, Pa dutifully carried home the tiny roast, and ate light that evening.

Even from across the sea Pa and Moofy found ways to continue hands-on grandparenting. Moofy invented a leprechaun named Trevor and wrote stories about him. These were read to and by all the children and grandchildren. The little grandchildren especially liked Trevor. Talking on the telephone to them, the children asked Moofy and Pa to send them a leprechaun. Moofy agreed. As soon as she was off the phone she found an empty shoe box, wrapped it up and sent Pa to the Post Office. When he handed the mysterious package to the clerk she looked a little perplexed.

"What's in there?" she asked, gently shaking the obviously empty box. Pa leaned a little closer to her and quietly answered,

"A leprechaun...for the grandchildren."

She gave him an understanding smile, and proceeded to weigh the package - leprechaun and all.

When they arrived in the States for their first furlough, Pa and Moofy went right away to the Missions Office to take care of some business. When they opened the front door, the receptionist switched on the intercom and announced, "Lord Pa and Lady Moofy have entered the building." I think that statement, made in fun, was more descriptive than the receptionist realized.

I know there are scores of people who would gladly give credit to Pa and Moofy for helping them through a milestone in their life. The godly counsel, advice, examples, and teaching received from them have helped turn lives to Christ, save marriages, return prodigals, encourage the down trodden, and confirm the righteous. As the apostle Paul said in I Corinthians 3:10:

> *"According to the grace of God which is given unto me, as a wise master builder, I have laid the foundation, and another buildeth thereon. But let every man take heed how he buildeth thereupon."*

My parents have worked hard to enter into the building of people's lives for the glory of God. I think many would say with me. . .

"Lord Pa and Lady Moofy have entered the building."

The End

My Family: Me, husband Ken, Eli and Rachel around 1993

Epilogue

Many people have had similar struggles to those Moofy and Pa dealt with. If you are dealing with an emptiness or longing in your life, Jesus Christ is the answer. He can do for you everything He did for Pa and Moofy. He can fill your life with abundant joy. The way you receive this gift of fulfillment is by accepting God's simple plan of salvation. John 3:16 says, "For God so loved the world, that he gave his only begotten Son, that whosoever believeth in him should not perish, but have everlasting life." That means that God loves you, too. He loves you so much He sent His Son to die on the cross to pay the ultimate penalty for your sins, and mine.

Romans 6:23 says, "For the wages of sin is death; but the gift of God is eternal life through Jesus Christ our Lord." That means that the wages we deserve to receive for the sins we commit is our own spiritual death which refers to an eternity in hell. But God offers a gift of eternal life with Him in heaven. All we have to do to receive that gift is admit to the fact that we are a sinner, and accept the gift of Jesus Christ.

Romans 3:23 says, "For all have sinned, and come short of the glory of God." So if you think you are not a sinner, think again. The Bible says that all are sinners because all have sinned. And we just saw that sin deserves eternal damnation in hell. But do you remember the part about the gift? Admitting that you are a sinner is the first step.

Now for the next step.

Romans 10:9-10 says, "That if thou shalt confess with thy mouth the Lord Jesus, and shalt believe in thine heart that God hath raised him from the dead, thou shalt be saved. For with the heart man believeth unto righteousness; and with the mouth confession is made unto salvation." Verse 13 then says, "For whosoever shall call upon the name of the Lord shall be saved." Step two is believing in your heart that Jesus died for your sins and is able and eager to forgive you. Step three is praying to God and telling Him that you know you are a sinner, you believe that Jesus died for your sins, and that you want to accept His free gift of salvation and become a child of God. At that point, your sins will be forgiven and God's Holy Spirit will come to live within you and you will belong to Him for eternity.

If you will follow this plan of salvation your life will change forever. God loves you and wants to be your Savior. Please allow Him to take charge of your life.